THE FIRST CLAIM...

a framework for
playwork quality assessment

'The right to play is a child's first claim on
the community. Play is nature's training for life.
No community can infringe that right
without doing deep and enduring harm to
the minds and bodies of it's citizens.'

David Lloyd George

Extracts from reviews of The First Claim

"This publication does exactly what it says in the sub-title. It makes no claim to assure quality, but instead it provides a mechanism to assess it, focusing on the play experiences of children and the role of the playworker.

The book provides a clear rationale for playwork and an extremely articulate description of what it is."

"It is a precise publication: the language is carefully chosen and strikes an excellent balance between shrouding the processes of play and playwork in new academic words and oversimplifying core concepts which might lead to misunderstanding."

"Finally, here is a publication with clout that gives playworkers the tools to articulate a playwork-based response to social policy agendas which threaten the child's right to play. It is provocative and challenging, it makes sense, it has potential to rescue playwork."

Play Today July 2001

Reviewed by Wendy Russell, playwork trainer and consultant

A Refreshing Look at Self-Assessment -

"Educationalists have been bombarded for years now with different forms of assessment of their work. . . . . . .

. . . . .How refreshing therefore in this environment to come across a brilliant form of self-assessment developed in one of the most difficult areas of educational practice to measure – playwork. The First Claim . . . . represents the very best of a profession establishing its peer led criteria for assessment and levels of performance. It sets benchmarks by which all other quality assurance schemes can be measured.

"The First Claim creates a superb model for education, whether informal or formal, to emulate."

"This subtle and refined assessment framework by colleagues in Wales is not just important because it has produced a valuable product which will aid play workers from initial volunteers to more experienced part-time staff, it is important because of its organic, peer-led process of construction and testing. It is the profession speaking and asserting itself without the impositions of removed bureaucracies and inappropriate frameworks linked to agendas removed from the needs of children."

"This . . . . . puts fun back into early years education and practitioners back in the driving seat."

RAPPORT, Journal of CYWU (The Union for Play, Youth and Community Workers): January 2002

Doug Nicholls. General Secretary CYWU

"Essential reading for professional playworkers and a necessary component for all training-book lists"

PlayRights - an international journal of the theory and practice of play: Sept 2001

PLAY WALES / CHWARAE CYMRU

PLAY WALES / CHWARAE CYMRU is the national organisation for children's play in Wales, funded by the National Assembly for Wales.

Play Wales was established in 1988 by the Welsh Office as a non-departmental public body hosted by the Welsh Association of District Councils, to increase awareness and understanding about the importance of children's play and to develop good quality local play opportunities for the children of Wales. In 1997, in response to an invitation from Win Griffiths, Minister for Children in Wales, Play Wales was re-established as a national charity.

The role of Play Wales is to influence policy, strategic planning and practice of all agencies and organisations that have an interest in, and a responsibility for children's play. This is achieved by providing information, technical advice and guidance: helping to identify needs and contributing to the increasing recognition of the profound importance of play as a critical component of children's development. Play Wales provides a forum for Playwork within the principality, and undertakes a national representational role for Playwork. This is achieved through:

- informing and consulting play organisations, workers, parents and children regarding new developments and initiatives;

- encouraging the introduction and implementation of policies for play, by local authorities and voluntary organisations throughout Wales;

- contributing to education and training and promoting good quality and safe practice in all aspects of children's play provision.

Play Wales encourages and supports the establishment of local, regional and national networks and supports the development of partnerships between statutory and voluntary organisations to improve co-ordination.

Services offered by Play Wales include:

- information, advice and consultancy service on all aspects of play provision

- advice and training on the content and implementation of play policies and strategies

- review of the quality and effectiveness of existing play provision

- safety inspections and risk assessment of existing play areas, adventure playgrounds and other staffed provision

- advice on design, location and content of playgrounds and planning policy

- training in the maintenance and management of play areas

- advice and assistance with litigation cases

- an information service providing publications, examples of practice, different provision and training materials

- seminars and conferences

- promotion of children's rights.

CONTENTS

PREFACE

Over the past few years it has appeared to me that as we have attempted to consider quality in playwork, we have tended to focus on what was tangible, more easily understood and issues that shared common ground with related professions. Thus today we have a number of quality assurance procedures that focus, in the main upon child protection and health and safety practice, and more recently suggested outcomes of our work.

However I have for long, believed that it is not what we do, but the way that we do it that makes playwork the unique process it is. However many of us have struggled with both the lack of concepts and a shared language with which to describe what we do and why, but possibly more importantly what we don't do and why we don't. In 'the first claim' we have tried to encapsulate the concepts we share and describe what we mean by the words we use in the context of children's play and playwork. The development of "the first claim" has been informed by scientific literature and encompasses the evolutionary, adaptational and therapeutic aspects of play.

As playworkers we are privileged to work with children in an (ideally) judgement free way. We are not parents, relatives or teachers in positions of conferred authority but 'merely' adults in the child's environment and if our practice is as effective as we can make it, then there is a unique opportunity for the most honest of relationships with the children with whom we work.

In 'the first claim' we have tried to explore the empathic affective reaction of playworkers with the children with whom they work - not just assessing the quality of our playwork with children but also where, as the playworker, we are coming from. To be truly effective we need to focus not just on practice but also on the source of our practice.

From the outset I was conscious that what we produced should incorporate a process that wasn't perceived as yet more work of limited relevance, but a process that clearly demonstrated that we can become more effective at what we do, something that is fun, (I'm not entirely sure we've achieved the latter), and a resource that could be used in virtually any context where children's play might be facilitated by the adult as a playworker.

When we consider the framework, it is at first sight beguiling in its simplicity, but upon analysis, when we apply it to our work, there is a surprising complexity. Whilst there was a desire to keep the framework as simple as possible, we recognised that many of the principles are necessarily complex and it will only take so much simplification without losing it's meaning.

Many of those involved in the development of 'the first claim', including myself, have commented upon the near immediate impact this work has had upon both our understanding and practice. It is as if we have undertaken a paradigm shift in our thinking. We recognise that 'the first claim' is a departure from the orthodoxy of quality assurance and is, in that respect experimental. However I am aware that it might also represent a watershed for playwork, the process, unlike others focusing not on what might be termed a 'legislative' model but upon play and the facilitation of play. As a professional playworker this is the tool I always needed.

For myself participating in this project has been a voyage of personal discovery, revisiting both my childhood and parenthood. I hope that all using this resource will share the same experience.

And finally, when using "The First Claim" we hope that people will not cherry pick, so as to speak - a great deal of thought, time and energy has gone into the totality of "The First Claim" and we believe that it would be diminished by dismemberment.

As we mention throughout, we hope to receive critical comment in order that we might most effectively develop this work, because ultimately this framework is predicated upon a simple question:.... 'what excuse do any of us have for not aspiring to excellence in playwork?'

Mike Greenaway
Director, Play Wales

FOREWORD

WHAT IS THE PROBLEM?
The theoretical/philosophical background

Given the perspective of human history as a whole, it is only in relatively recently times that adult society has felt it necessary to designate specific spaces in which children can play.

This has happened mainly for reasons of safety - safety from traffic, from abduction and harm, and safety from hazards - and for the past thirty or so years, many adults have concluded that children's play needs are best served by ensuring they have access to specified play spaces, sometimes supervised and operated by playworkers, i.e. trained adults who have a high level of knowledge and experience of working with children in play situations.

However, whereas prior to this development the rationale and content of children's play would have been determined by the play drive of the children themselves, this is not necessarily the case now. For with the recent proliferation of supervised play spaces, many of the adults involved, including playworkers, their funders and managers and the children's parents, have begun to perceive the role of the playworker as increasingly interventionist, both in terms of what the children in their charge do and how they do it, when they are playing. This view has been particularly reinforced by recent safety, equal opportunities and anti-bullying perspectives.

Increased intervention has had two effects:

● to a greater or lesser extent, it has taken control of their play away from children

● adult control has replaced what might be an instinctive biological agenda with what could be termed an 'adulterated' or socialising agenda (Else and Sturrock, 1998).

Play is thought to be the visible result of a biological drive (Sturrock, 1993, Rennie and Sturrock, 1997). It has existed throughout human evolution, and is thought to be a significant factor in every aspect of human development - from co-ordination to language, and from brain development to adaptation. If this is true - and increasingly the evidence points in this direction - then it would be absolutely essential to all children's optimum development that they engage in high quality play experiences, for significant amounts of time each day, throughout the period of their childhood.

But because of the increase in adult intervention, the lives of many children are already partially or completely devoid of the adult-free experience which play should be. Furthermore, we do not know whether the impact of adult intervention is having any deleterious effect on this important and fragile process. Although, given the subtle and delicate nature of play, my fear is that inappropriate levels and types of intervention, for example, intervention that continually interrupts, changes, curtails or represses children's play behaviour, is acting as a pre-cursor to what may be a serious developmental crisis for many children.

The developmental crisis to which I refer could already be manifesting itself in one of three forms:

- a physical form, in which children, unable - because of constraints imposed by 'inappropriate' supervision - to adequately calibrate or co-ordinate their bodies, risk-assess or lay the complex foundations for language, meta-communication or other forms of social interaction, in ways in which they have previously been enabled through adult-free play

- an emotional form, where children - because of constraints imposed by 'inappropriate' supervision, are unable to make sense of what is happening to them and to the world around them in the contexts for example, of relationships, mortality, morality and religion

- a synthesis of both the physical and emotional forms.

To make matters worse - perhaps due to our currently litigious culture - concerns regarding safety are almost as prominent inside designated play spaces as they are outside them. This has led to concerns being raised regarding the suitability or appropriateness of allowing children to engage in a whole range of what would have in the past been regarded as legitimate play experiences.

The outcome is that adults are intentionally erasing certain types of play, in particular rough and tumble, some forms of social, creative, mastery and deep play from the everyday play experiences of many children. This would be serious enough if it only impacted on some of the available play time of the children affected. But increasingly, the play experience some children are getting in designated play spaces constitutes the only play they have. Thus in this context, particular children so affected could be suffering significant harm and developmental damage as a consequence of 'play deprivation'.

Although the whole area of quality in children's play has been the subject of considerable attention recently - particularly with regard to legislation and health and safety - very little regard has been paid either to children's play itself or to the most appropriate environmental or psychological conditions under which it might be facilitated.

To address this Play Wales has developed the frameworks that follow. Their purpose, being to enable playworkers and other concerned and interested adults to analyse, by observation and reflection, the play environments they operate - or that their children use - and assess the quality of what is being provided and experienced and to use that knowledge to explore:

- the nature of what the children are doing

- the possible developmental and therapeutic roles of playing

- the roles and functions of the playworker in facilitating play

- the most appropriate modes of intervening in the play process

- the language and concepts of playwork.

Play is a very complicated phenomenon, and not surprisingly playwork, i.e. work with playing children is equally complex. Each child is not only a social individual with needs and rights of its own, s/he is a developmental universe whose personal fulfilment is dependent upon an interaction with a wide range of subtle factors that cannot easily be described in empirical forms.

Because of this, the frameworks contained within the following pages generally describe principles rather than facts. These principles, for example, the notion of play as 'freely chosen, personally directed and intrinsically motivated behaviour', have been derived using a synthesis of experience from a whole variety of sources including playworker's intuition, their childhood memories, their professional playwork experiences and the existing scientific literature on play.

These principles may be construed by some as inconvenient, unrealistic, idealistic, unconventional or even irrelevant when applied to current forms of provision and some current 'styles' of playwork. But our deepest consideration in their development is not whether children will fit into the provision we make and the playwork that takes place there, but rather whether either the provision or the playwork addresses the child's play needs as far as we understand them. There certainly exists some tension in some play provision between the construct of play as identified in the literature, the contemporary play experience which is alluded to in these processes and playwork as practised in some settings.

This tension may exist as a result of training, (see Hughes, (1997b), which may have over-emphasised issues like legislation and other factors like socialisation and behavioural management, whilst under-emphasised the importance of play's role in the development and adaptation of our species. Whatever the source of the dissonance between knowledge and practice it is important that playworkers are able to look at their practice, and come to a personal assessment of the quality of what they do from the perspective of what play is and does. The playwork criteria contained within the Play Wales frameworks will enable that by providing playworkers with comparative reference points derived from the sources referred to above.

The two frameworks contained within this resource - BASIC and INTERMEDIATE - and the third - ADVANCED - which will eventually accompany them, may best be viewed as increasingly detailed playwork maps, which by identifying some of the main features of the playwork and play landscapes can help playworkers to navigate the most appropriate paths too and from them.

The frameworks also provide us with what Sturrock, (1999) calls 'a North', enabling playworkers to make certain qualitative judgements in relation to the experiences, (the sum of the environmental and intervention experiences), they offer children in the different forms of provision they operate. In addition, we anticipate that over time and with an increasingly informed and rigorous debate, authentic standard will begin to evolve from these frameworks.

The frameworks have been developed by playworkers for use by playworkers, rather than by managers or inspectors in the first instance. They have been piloted in a variety of settings to ensure that they are as relevant to current day provision and practice as is possible without compromising playwork's fundamental characteristics. Thus ensuring that the main thrust of the playworker's practice is focused on the play needs of children rather than on the social and vocational needs of their parents, guardians and carers.

We have developed these frameworks with two main objectives. The first is that they will ensure that children who use the spaces playworkers operate get access to the best play service possible, and the second is that the use of these frameworks will enable the playworker to provide that.

Bob Hughes, Process Co-ordinator
Autumn 2000

SECTION 1 - INTRODUCTION
PLAYWORK QUALITY ASSESSMENT

What Is Playwork Quality Assessment?

Playwork Quality Assessment is a process, for improving the quality of children's play experiences in a range of play settings and thereby assuring the highest quality of experiences for children in those settings. It builds on the evolving knowledge and experience of playworkers in a variety of settings. It aims to continue the process of deepening playworkers knowledge and expertise with the objective of creating the right environment in which children can play freely and develop.

The Purpose Of Quality Assessment

The purpose of quality assessment for any service is that as well as being able to demonstrate to parents, the general public, funders and legal and regulatory bodies, that it operates within an agreed set of standards, that provision is also addressing the developing play needs of the children who use it in a manner which whilst emphasising respect for children's integrity and sensitivity to the fragile nature of the play process, also reflects contemporary understanding of the importance of play and the mechanisms of the play process. In this specific context it is also intended to demonstrate that the notion of quality itself is a vital but often neglected concept.

1 WHY DO WE NEED PLAYWORK QUALITY ASSESSMENT?

This framework has been developed because it was felt that much of the play and playwork training currently available to the field has lost its focus on 'children' and 'play', and has instead become a process for satisfying the requirements of legal and regulatory bodies - i.e. one which whilst it addresses adult concerns, does not see the play - and as a consequence the developmental - needs of children, as at least of equal, if not greater importance, in a society in which 'the child's needs' are deemed of paramount importance. The framework is intended to redress that imbalance.

The framework is primarily focused on the child and its specific play needs rather than on concerns about how many fire extinguishers are in a building or whether the sink has been cleaned today. For whilst the legal and regulatory elements have obvious importance, there is a recognised range of information and training already available to cover them, whereas there are few, if any systems of this kind that focus entirely on the play needs of children and the appropriateness or otherwise of the adult input within that context.

Thus our intention is that **this framework should complement other quality assessment systems** and training and education opportunities currently available, rather than duplicating them.

External Influences

There currently exists a number of legal and regulatory requirements or standards, which relate to the range of provision in which children are supervised when they are playing. With this framework, we aim to provide the tools for reasoned arguments for ensuring children's play experiences are not compromised through over zealous or rigid interpretations of other standards, legal or regulatory requirements, offering instead a common sense approach to play and playwork.

Quality Assessment Systems

Many quality assurance systems are intended to simply record and evaluate information on a periodic basis. However, as we developed this work we felt that a quality assessment framework for children's play should also attempt to provide a number of graduated tools which over time would have the cumulative effect of:

- improving playworker's knowledge and practice

- improving play experiences for children

- ensuring practice does not cause harm to children

- helping parents and others to understand the meaning and purpose of quality play provision

- enabling projects to attract funding by demonstrating project's high levels of understanding and practice

- influencing day-care registration and inspection

- upgrading the professionalism of playworkers

- providing a continuous improvement and development process.

- contributing to the improvement and updating of the content of playwork training and education

- demonstrating a commitment to quality play processes

- having over time a cumulative effect which enabled the allocation of resources for dedicated spaces.

1 THE PURPOSE OF THE FRAMEWORK

This quality assessment framework has been designed to give playworkers and play providers an opportunity to explore, reflect on and develop their practice and the provision within which that practice takes place.

Its key purpose is to improve the quality of the play experience and play opportunities, which are made available to children.

This framework is intended to be of value wherever staffed play provision exists, whether individuals are employed or volunteers; whether provision is full-time year-round or part-time sessional; closed-access childcare or open-access playwork, in fact anywhere that children might play, regardless of the context.

The framework provides guidance for playworkers to understand and identify what is quality play, and importantly, what is quality playwork. It is intended to enable playworkers to refresh their perspective of their work by highlighting the unique nature:

- of the playworker's relationship with the children s/he serves

- of the interactive relationship the child has with the physical and emotional environment s/he is playing in.

The framework provides a systematic approach for playworkers to be able to organise their work, and through continuous development, its use is intended to become common practice in the workplace.

The framework contains numerous complex concepts that may be new to some. However, they are grounded in the observations of playworkers currently engaged in face-to-face work. Understanding these complex concepts, observing them in the daily practice of playwork, planning, recording and reflecting on them, will help all of us engaged in playwork to raise our standards of service delivery and provide increasingly relevant and appropriate play experiences for children.

The complete Playwork Quality Assessment framework will evolve over a period of time. There will be three elements to the overall system. These are:

- Self Assessment for individual playworkers

- Peer Assessment where colleagues assess each other's practice

- External Assessment where an independent body of expert practitioners assess practice and provision.

BUT LET'S BE CLEAR what we're talking about in this framework is SELF ASSESSMENT.

1 WHO IS THE FRAMEWORK FOR?

playworkers: it will take each individual on a journey through their playwork practice, and help them plan for their future by identifying strengths, locating sources of further information and recognising their training needs.

Who else will benefit?

managers: it will re-emphasise the importance and value of play and playwork. It will also provide a tool for assessing quality, which will contribute to Best Value.

parents: although the pack and processes are primarily intended to lead to a higher standard of playwork input for their children, it will also increase their awareness and understanding of the importance of quality play experiences to their children's life-long development.

day-care registration and inspection officers: it is intended that this framework will be useful in developing an increased understanding of play and playwork issues and help them to develop common standards. The information gathered during the quality assessment process can also be used to facilitate other assessment and inspection.

funders: it will enable funders to have a clearer understanding of playworkers' and play providers' needs and the value of quality play provision. In addition, it will demonstrate the importance of supporting the continued development of playwork services.

training and education providers: it is envisaged that over time the criteria used, and their definitions and descriptions will affect the future content of training and education received both by new and experienced playworkers. Ultimately, it is intended to raise the status and professionalism of all playworkers.

2

SECTION 2 - RISK
RISKS IN A CHILD'S BEHAVIOUR

What follows invites us all to reflect upon the need for children to be exposed to certain types of risk, to encounter it, assess it and develop skills to manage it. It is considered to be an essential part of the whole process of confidence and competence building, necessary for personal development and survival.

Why risk is an important and integral part of play

By pursuing a wide range of experiences, activities and behaviour in their play, children have the opportunity to discover their limitations and realise their potential for doing things. The variety of opportunities available to them will determine to a large extent the type of human being they will later become. A paucity of stimulating play experiences will clearly not be of value in the development of a confident, happy and resourceful human being.

Risk encounter and subsequent risk assessment and management is clearly associated with a number of play process mechanisms mentioned within this Quality Assessment framework. These include combinatorial flexibility, co-ordination, deep play, exploratory play and mastery play.

We believe that facilitating each of these mechanisms is profoundly important if children are to benefit from playing in supervised play environments.

Virtually all aspects of play present an element of physical or psychological risk to children, to a lesser or greater degree. From birth children are inquisitive and curious with an innate and compelling drive to explore the unknown, to experiment, to test themselves against numerous physical parameters and to establish their personal position within the social and non-social environments.

Play is the most natural process within which such development is enhanced. Access to a wide variety of opportunities is therefore crucial if we are to ensure that children are exposed to a comprehensive learning experience. By coming into contact with graduated risk taking situations in a controlled environment, children will develop a capacity to identify, assess and manage other activities with risk content. This whole process we argue, is related to the survival instinct. It is built on the premise that physical and intellectual competence initially encourages confidence and subsequently an ability to cope with difficulties presented in the wider world.

It is abundantly clear that children and parents consider it is more favourable for children to discover risk management skills in a supervised play environment rather than in other everyday life situations. Additionally, the risk management skills developed through play may be seen by parents to be of greatest benefit for children when they are playing in the street or other open environments.

In addition to the above it is believed that graduated levels of risk should be recognised as being of creative importance in the evolving play process. We would argue that in order for children to develop risk management skills in the playwork setting there needs to be a fundamental change in operational practices, the attitudes of playworkers and the enforcement of strict safety regimes. The imposition of which often contradict the very essence and ethos of play.

Stimulation versus Safety

The ever increasing concern among the public at large about the safety of children has prompted the introduction of a range of controls and conditions which at times appear to overwhelm managers of provision and indeed children themselves.

As a direct consequence of the introduction of controls and conditions, the ranges and patterns of play behaviour have been somewhat restricted and there has been an increasing leaning towards safety measures rather than the comprehensive play experience. The opportunity for children to express the full extent of their play knowledge has therefore been more and more constricted. Clearly this has limited the children's opportunity to develop a capacity to confront and subsequently manage risk.

It is our considered view that the outcome of a more rigidly controlled play environment will result in children being unable to deal with hazardous situations themselves in later life. Consequently there is a real likelihood that accident and injury will increase because of the lack of confidence and the skill necessary to deal with risk scenarios.

Lost knowledge

It must also be remembered that the children who are being denied the opportunity to experience and manage risk may soon become parents themselves. The very real danger is that the risk management skills that are so necessary for children's survival and development will be lost to the next generation, as the parents of the future will not have developed the skills or knowledge to pass on.

As with parents so it is with playworkers. Unless there is a fundamental shift in the mentality of playworkers to recognise the need for risk in play, future generations of playworkers will also be unable to pass on the appropriate risk management experiences, strategies and skills.

Playwork - the passive profession

We recognise that it is easy for the play profession to glibly condemn this misperceived public concern as an over reaction to media hype and scare mongering. However this remains a major issue for a huge number of parents, professionals and the children themselves. And an issue that as a profession we have not even begun to successfully address.

Whilst we hope that the issues raised in this paper will resonate with a large number of play professionals and enable them to reflect on their own practice we do not think that is enough. It is the responsibility of everyone in the play field to encourage appropriate risk in play; to take time to convince parents and professionals in other fields that the way the play opportunity operates, contains a realisation that risk is a fundamental part of the process of human development.

In practical terms this means that playworkers, play managers, local authorities and insurers are going to have to accept the fact that accidents will happen, that children will sometimes hurt themselves when they play.

Knowledge and Risk

We are not saying that the playworker bears no responsibility to ensure safety. Of course it is right that playworkers should seek to identify and take action to avoid preventable accidents that will result in injury to children. However there is considerable concern that play provision has an excessive focus on removing all potential risk situations. We feel this is not only unrealistic but also potentially disabling for children.

Clearly young children are not able to perceive risks to the extent that adults are. But unless they are allowed to confront different levels of risk in a supervised context they will be denied the opportunity to develop their capacity for anticipating and recognising risk.

All children need to discover their ability to manage their own bodies in relation to space, physical objects, environmental features and characteristics, materials and indeed other people. They need to explore the emotional and intellectual risks of childhood, to learn and understand that they can make mistakes and not have them looked at as though they are major disasters or indeed actions which belittle their status.

2

Through progressive risk taking processes, children will develop the practical life skills so essential to them later on. In achieving this, playworkers must identify what sensible steps and appropriate measures need to be introduced in relation to the behaviour and characteristics of individual children.

In addressing this issue we advocate a more sensible approach to safety. Our starting point is that play behaviour must come first and that safety conditions must be applied in a measured, incremental and responsive manner rather than through a rigid and dogmatic regime. The new approach needs to be based on the playworker's knowledge and experience of:

● the child's behaviour in relation to the exact set of circumstances they are operating in at that time

● the play environment and the community in which it functions

● children's behaviour at different stages of growth and development

● the history and experience of accidents in relation to equipment and environment, and different types of activity

● the playworker's ability to understand the capability of children when encountering risk.

Whilst playworkers have a responsibility to ensure the general safety of the play environment there is a need to create opportunities for children to explore and control their own parameters. They should be allowed to determine their own route through a range of experiences within which they are measuring and testing their capacity to manage risk by adopting or adapting responses to it. The playworker is there to assist, guide and support children through that process.

One of the central areas that the playworker needs to be aware of, as part of the risk management process is the ability of children to undertake their own risk management. At play children develop an increasing awareness of their capacity for doing things.

The worker's assessment of the child's abilities to undertake an activity that has elements of risk is made at the time, within the particular circumstances that exist.

2

There can be no generic risk management protocol i.e. 'it is OK for nine year olds to undertake this activity but not seven year olds...' It may only be acceptable for that particular nine year old to undertake that activity at that time. It may not be appropriate for the same individual to undertake the activity at another time.

However, this process of enabling children to access risk does assume that the common sense procedures of removing all obvious dangers have been completed.

Although always important, the issue of risk management becomes even more critical when children are participating in 'deep play'. (Hughes, 1996a) This particular play type is essential for a child's personal development. Deep play means that children engage in play, which enables them to explore their own range of abilities, develop survival skills and experience fear and the conquest of fear. On the face of it when adults observe children taking part in deep play they may perceive it to be extremely dangerous and even life threatening.

However, in our experience, children who are immersed in deep play are able to do so because of having already experienced a graduated process of risk taking and risk management, and are extremely self-confident and competent at play, possessing an understanding of their capacity for managing risk.

SECTION 3 - THE PROCESS
SELF-ASSESSMENT FOR QUALITY PLAYWORK PRACTICE

It is not yet possible to allocate specific empirical standards to playwork (and for that matter is it desirable) as most of the concepts and ideas in use are currently undergoing exploration and development. However, if a play environment feels right to children, i.e. if playworkers are engaging with the space and the children using it appropriately, and if it offers children particular types of experiences, then through a free interaction with certain props, it will stimulate the appearance of high quality play behaviour indicators.

There is emerging evidence that high quality play experiences inhibit the effects of play deprivation, facilitate neurological development, heighten neuro-chemical activity, and enable the development of skills essential to a child's physical and mental well-being.

We can only ensure that children experience high quality play by making qualitative judgements about **what, as playworkers, we do** and **how, as playworkers, we do it**, and by asking, **is our practice better enabling children to play**?

What we do is about providing the props necessary to stimulate play, through a process called 'environmental modification', i.e. by adapting the physical and psychological characteristics of the play environment to better suit the needs of the children using it.

How we do it, is about ensuring that we apply 'appropriate intervention styles' and, by so doing, facilitate particular behavioural modes. If the props, intervention styles and behavioural modes we apply do enable play, we will be able to see that happening by the appearance of Indicators of Play Behaviours and Mood Descriptors.

Play is the term we use to describe how a child engages with the world in its own way and for its own reasons. To help us to identify the most appropriate props, intervention styles and behavioural modes for children to do this we need to identify the various environmental components that most effectively enable play to occur.

We recognise that the play settings in which playworkers find themselves vary greatly and understand that not all settings have the physical characteristics available to enable children to play with and interact with all of the components as listed below and as described in the Ideas and Terminology sections of the individual framework parts.

However, feedback from playworkers in a variety of settings suggests that there is scope to think creatively about the opportunities to play with the different props that are available to the children we work with. There is a space provided in each process for playworkers - who having thought broadly about what they offer - to give specific examples of play in their settings. One playworker, for example, gave candle making as an example of fire play.

We should add, that where you feel that the explanations and examples given in the Ideas and Terminology sections are unclear or inadequate, it is important that this is fed back into the developmental process by notifying Play Wales.

3 PREPARING FOR SELF-ASSESSMENT

The framework for self-assessment is in three parts. BASIC, INTERMEDIATE, and the ADVANCED framework. Each part will be undertaken consecutively. To attempt each part you will need to do a number of things.

1. First of all, you will need to familiarise yourself with each part in turn. Thinking about the terminology and reading the accompanying 'Definitions and Explanations' sections. Take your time over this.

2. Secondly, it will be helpful if you spend some time, say 1/4-1/2 hour to start with, observing the children you work with, actually playing, reflecting on what they are doing and what the self-assessment process is asking about.

3. Then you should work on each part of the self-assessment process until you are familiar with that part of the total process and feel that the results you arriving at are a fair and accurate reflection of the quality of what you do judged against your understanding of the principles implied in the various questions.

4. Ideally each part of the framework will be completed by you whilst you are observing the children playing (or as soon afterwards as possible).

When you are able confidently to undertake, for example, the BASIC assessment and have a clear idea about any subsequent changes you may need to make in your knowledge or practice as a result, move onto the next level of complexity, i.e., the INTERMEDIATE assessment.

The third of the Three Graduated QA Options will be an ADVANCED QA Framework. This procedure will be incorporated at a later date.

Note

Some playworkers, particularly those who work in more enclosed, poorly resourced or part-time situations may feel that the frameworks are aimed at purpose-built adventure playgrounds and the full-time workers who operate them, rather than at themselves. This is certainly not intended to be the case. However, the process does have to assess quality as a whole and is therefore intended to reflect our current understanding of the complete spectrum of play experiences children need for their successful development. It is intended that the frameworks should apply to anyone who works with children in any context where play may or should take place.

Inescapably some of these will be 'outdoor', 'unrestrained' and sometimes 'risky' experiences simply because in normal circumstances they would be a typical part of children's everyday play. Having said that however, we should also remember that the success of supervised play provision does not only rely on the quality of the environment children have to interact with and the experiences they can access there. All the physical

resources in the world can be destroyed by poor interaction between the child and playworker. That is why, throughout this process, the primary focus - once the bottom line of the essential range of experience, (which does include outdoor play, fire and risk, for example), has been established - is on the way playworkers interact with the children and the perceived knowledge and value base that underpins these interaction and interventions.

Unavoidably, some playworkers will score low Grades. This may be because their provision or practice does fall below an acceptable 'bottom-line'. If this is so, it is in the interest of the playworker to know this, if for no other reason than it gives them the opportunity to change that situation both, for the benefit of the children for whom the provision exists and for their own professional satisfaction.

There will also be those who are intuitively aware that what they do can and should be improved, but have no evidence to use to demonstrate a need for training or an improvement in provision to managers or funders. This self-assessment framework will provide them with tangible guidance of what is expected and any shortfalls that should be addressed. It is intended to be a tool that enables the identification of excellence and/or mediocrity and promote reflection, so that practice can be improved.

We believe that having access to high quality play experiences as described within the self-assessment framework is not only essential to the healthy development of all children in Wales, it is their right. Thus where provision is not currently able to satisfy these proposed standards, whether for reasons of funding, training, siting, staffing or whatever, we see it as our responsibility to address these deficits with commitment and energy because of the serious impact they may be having on the overall developmental capacity and potential of the children affected.

3 GRADING

One of the main benefits of this framework is that it enables playworkers to grade their practice according to their assessment of the knowledge, understanding and skills they have. This provides a vital starting point for the development of a collective view, both of what criteria constitute quality, but also at what point quality benchmarks can be established.

The grading process is intended to be very straightforward. By simply responding to questions about your practice - in terms of the environment you have created; how you interact with the children; your style of intervention and your depth of understanding of the children's behaviour - you are able to award yourself points ranging from 1-4 depending upon the responses you give. At the end of the assessment the points are added up, and where the points match a particular grade range, that grade corresponds to the current the qualitative grade you have assessed for your practice.

In the Basic Framework the total points possible in each level of assessment is divided into four equal groups, of 25 points. Each of these groups is allocated a grade and the following scores apply to the following grades and mean the following:

Grade 1 (76 - 100) Your understanding and practice needs very little attention in any area

Grade 2 (51 - 75) Your understanding and practice needs some attention in a few areas

Grade 3 (26 - 50) Your understanding and practice needs significant attention in some areas

Grade 4 (0 - 25) Your understanding and practice needs considerable attention in all areas

The Intermediate Framework has a greater number of points; reflecting the increased number of elements to be considered, however the grading principle is the same as the basic.

We also want the assessment to acknowledge that playworkers have to operate under wildly differing, and sometime very difficult conditions. Therefore, in the BASIC and INTERMEDIATE sections, when you have completed your initial assessment you will come to a section called "Factors that militate against quality". The procedure here is just slightly different to the previous one. This part of the assessment asks you whether you feel that certain factors have a negative impact upon your ability to operate. For example, does the area your provision is sited in make it difficult for you to do your job, or does the level of racism in the area make playwork difficult? Where you judge that the listed factors have a significant affect on your practice, tick the appropriate box and award yourself half a point for each ticked box.

To reach your amended grade, simply add the 'factors that militate against quality' points to your earlier total and change the grade accordingly.

3

These quality assessment frameworks are intended to make it possible to:

● form the basis of a review of the provision you make and your own and your team's practice within it

● identify areas in your understanding of play and playwork where you judge that you would benefit from additional training and support

● identify areas in your practice where you would benefit from additional training and support, particularly in the context of intervention, empathic absorption and adulteration.

Note that whilst in the BASIC process you are asked to assess your practice on a 'Never, Sometimes, Often, Normally', basis, for the INTERMEDIATE process the term 'Never', is replaced with 'Rarely'. This shift emphasises the expectation of the process that practice and awareness is improving and that whilst at a BASIC level certain features may be omitted without practice being upgradeable, this will not be the case at either the INTERMEDIATE or ADVANCED levels.

The Results

These frameworks are designed to provide playworkers with two distinct insights. The most obvious of these is that having used the frameworks, self-assessed their practice and over time come to a grade which they feel accurately and authentically reflects the relative quality of what they do, that they will be clearer about what playwork is and what is meant by quality playwork practice. They will also have a more considered view of their professional training needs.

However, we expect other affects too. Affects that have a great deal more to do with the playworker than with playwork practice.

For too long playworkers have been expected - or have expected themselves - to do what is a difficult and demanding job with little or no reference to who they are, from a playwork perspective, or to the impact that playwork has on them.

For example, little reference has ever been given to the affect of transference on playworkers. The impact of interfacing - sometimes over many years - with hundreds, perhaps thousands of children many of whom may be seriously damaged.

Neither has playwork shown any particular interest in the childhood play experiences of playworkers themselves. This is serious. For if playworkers have had restricted and repressed play experiences themselves, for example, it should not be surprising if the provision they make, either reflects that, or is some way acts as a compensation for it.

Thus as well as exploring the quality of the experiences playworkers are making available to the children with whom they work, these processes are also intended to stimulate the practice of reflection and discourse about the quality of the experiences playworkers have had and are having, as another route to enabling improvements in practice to take place.

When playworkers begin to apply these processes to the environments in which they work and to the way in which they interface with children who use them, we also predict that some of the following effects and affects will occur:

1. Playworkers will begin to absorb and use the language this framework contains because it will enable a level of communication between playworkers about playwork concepts and practice that has until now has not been available.

2. Playworkers will experience anger, and perhaps as a result frustration, of stupidity or of realising how impoverished were their own childhood play experiences. If this occurs it is important that the playworker explores why this is happening.

3. Playworkers will become more conscious of their potential to adulterate children's play.

4. Playworkers will initially experience fear. Fear that their practice is inadequate or that they do not have the skills to be a playworker. Again, it is important that if this is the playworker's initial reaction that s/he explore why this is so. This is a particular challenge to playworkers who are also parents.

5. Playworkers will experience what Kent Palmer called, 'an ecstasy of variety'; the feeling one gets when in a truly playful space.

The Language

This is a vital development. Imagine architects or doctors being unable to talk to each other conceptually about the work on which they are engaged. Imagine engineering or mathematics without their own language. Conceptual languages applying to specific disciplines - as far as we understand them - do not exist to exclude people but to bind those people together who need that language for the purposes of scholarship and excellence in practice.

A playwork language to communicate the concepts and ideas particular to playwork should be no exception. However, because its primary purpose is to enable those who see playwork as a means of facilitating complex biological mechanisms - about which we only currently have the glimmerings of understanding - it does by its very nature contain the jargon characteristic of any technical language.

What, for example, is combinatorial flexibility, and to what does it refer? Coined initially by Bruner, (1972) and Sylva, (1977), only the vaguest of explanations is given in scientific terms. And yet to the playworker - observing and appreciating, as s/he does in daily practice the breathtaking changes and abilities of children who come to play spaces to interact and to explore - the notion that the human child's brain is both equipped to, and capable of computing and permutation of packets of experience at high speed, in order to solve what are new problems for the child, is not a revelation, although understanding the mechanisms may be.

Those who do not allow themselves to be repelled by new terminology will quickly discover that its challenge is not to their intelligence or to the quality of their practice, but rather to their own professional satisfaction. For it asks, 'As playworkers are we really doing the best we can?', in a language in which reflection is unavoidable. No longer need we be guided only by legislation, or policies designed for adults or fear of litigation.

Anger

Anger from Frustration

Some playworkers will experience anger. If anger is your reaction to these Quality Assessment processes it is important that you explore why this is happening. The BASIC process for example poses a number of different challenges.

For example, if your playwork provides an environment with particular characteristics. Implicit here is the playing child's need for enrichment, for diversity, for compensation and risk. Anger may be generated by the perceived impossibility of the proposed task. We are all aware that playwork is a difficult, under-resourced and sometimes dangerous profession. We are also aware that all too often playworkers are expected to practice in cramped and sterile spaces, totally unsuited to the realities of a group of playing children.

Thus anger may be a reflection of a perceived mismatch between what you feel able to do and what you feel you are being asked to do. The mismatch may be real, in which case we will adjust the process. On the other hand anger may be a symptom of your own obstruction to change, and you will need to deal with that.

Anger from Perceived Stupidity

Alternatively, anger might be generated, not by the proposed task's impossibility, but by its perceived stupidity. Do children get to play with fire, it asks? Can they play with tools? If anger is the playworkers reaction, s/he should ask herself why? Is it so unreasonable to expect that children would normally be driven to play with fire or tools, given the opportunity? Certainly there are issues of safety inherent in such opportunities, but there are also issues of disability inherent in their prohibition. Children need to engage with the real world and one of playwork's implicit beliefs is that play is nature's medium for doing this. The issue for the playworker, when conditions are conducive, is not, why should I not ban this, but how can I enable it with the minimum of risk to children who may be new to such experiences.

Anger from 'Empathic Absorption'

However, anger may also be rooted in something altogether more serious. Working with children in any context can be draining - ask a parent, but working for long periods with children some of whom are perhaps distressed or damaged, in a context which by its very nature should be uncontrolled and child-centred, can, in some circumstances have a deleterious impact particularly on the playworker's mental well-being.

For playworkers - given their professional context and their in-depth knowledge of the children and their families - are extremely vulnerable to what might be termed 'empathic absorption'. - that is similar in nature to the psychotherapeutic term, 'transference'. Empathic absorption occurs where playworkers - perhaps because of the unique bonding that playwork creates - identify with and subconsciously absorb the imagined pain or distress of the children even though they themselves may have never experienced either the type of intensity or that negativity. The effect on playworkers of such absorption is that it could at least render them vulnerable to feelings of guilt and, if experienced over time, could render them traumatised and aggressive.

Naturally, if this absorption is occurring or has occurred; if we are injured ourselves by it, then to be expected to do any more - for example to fill in quality assessment forms, may be regarded as inappropriate. Again, this should be thought through, and, on reflection it may be prioritised as a training imperative in the future. You also wish to discuss this with a colleague.

Anger from Technical Dissection

Anger may also be associated with the pain stemming from the technical dissection, into its component parts, of a process that is felt to be highly personal and intimate. How could these people know about 'my play'; why don't they just emphasise fun and safety; do we need to know about play in such depth? But of course to a greater or lesser extent, that is exactly what playwork in general and these processes in particular are attempting to do - to improve our practice by broadening our knowledge and by deepening our reflections.

3

Anger from Impoverished Personal Experience

Some playworkers, like any other group of adults may have experienced impoverishment in their play. For example, play may have been a narrow or controlled experience for them. As a consequence they may, when using the processes, associate them with their own childhood experiences and feel emotion in the form of envy or jealousy. There may be those who in their childhood saw children burned by fire or injured with a tool, and in seeing play with fire and tools advocated in the processes, associate that with their own childhood experience and feel guilt or responsibility as a consequence.

In conversations between them, Sturrock and Hughes, describe this - using the psychotherapeutic term 'counter transference' - as a misfit between affect and context; that what is felt is inappropriate in the circumstances in which it is being felt. The playworker who truly reflects upon why they are feeling angry when anger is clearly inappropriate in that context, will uncover a number of answers to the question, Why do I feel angry?, which if analysed will reveal unrealised associations which can themselves be 'played out' or resolved by the affected playworker.

Adulteration

The other challenge offered by the process relates to the playworker's potential to control and adulterate children's play through their own intervention. Else and Sturrock, (1998), after Sturrock, (1997). cite adulteration as the, 'contamination of the play aims and objects of the children by either the wishes of the adult in an urge to 'teach' or 'educate', simply to dominate, or by the worker's own un-played out material'.

The playworkers function is to facilitate children's play. It is not to interrupt, control, manipulate, organise or in some way to dominate either the content or intent of what the children are doing. Consequently it is essential that any direct playful engagement or organisational prescription of what children do is kept to a minimum and even then it should be justifiable. The inclusion, in the framework, of several questions that refer to the nature of the interaction between playworker and children is a measure of how seriously adulteration is taken in this process.

3

For many children - particularly those who attend child-care provision - the play they experience there may constitute the great bulk of their total play input/output. This puts an onerous responsibility upon the quality of the playworkers practice. What should be considered is twofold. One, the powerful relationship between play and human development, and two the fact that play for many children in middle and late childhood should be an adult-free experience.

If children, for all sort of economic and social reasons have to attend childcare provision it is incumbent upon the playwork field to ensure that those children have the highest quality and most natural play experiences possible. That means, where possible, adult free experiences, and where not possible, experiences in which the adult is as non-intrusive, as non-influential in the play process as possible. Anything more moves on to a potential spectrum ranging from socialisation to indoctrination. In fact, we would go so far as to say that if children's play is continually adulterated, those children will be developmentally harmed.

Fear

For some the affect may initially be fear. That, for example, they are inadequate as playworkers and that their practice is poor. This is a natural reaction to what may be perceived as a complex new tool and any process that is intended to assist high quality will inevitably identify mediocrity. Having said that, the only reason that this framework is being developed at all is to help playworkers to be more effective in their work and to begin to identify their training needs. So although initial fear is an understandable emotion, the process is intended to replace that with a new professional confidence born out of increasing understanding of the play process and the practice of playwork.

Ecstasy

As is implied above we are conscious that there are powerful and inevitable affective links between the concepts and language used in each of the three levels of assessment, and our personal experiences of playing. And that for some, the concepts and language we use, may trigger only negative feelings.

However, for many others the emotions they feel will be a balance between the positive and negative. Whilst for others, the effect of absorbing and implementing the process will be what Kent Palmer called, 'an ecstasy of variety'; the feeling one gets when in a truly playful space or as Meares describes, 'a kind of day dreaming'. Playworkers have already reported that using this quality assessment framework, 'made me smile', that 'it has totally changed the way I see my job', and 'it has totally changed the way we work'.

This almost over-enthusiasm is as predictable as the negative view. For as well as containing events that generate fear, anger and unhappiness, play also contains experiences that generate intense and pleasurable emotions that the word fun hardly encapsulates. Ecstasy, a celebration of realisation, an induction into sensuality, contentment and joy are more fitting terms for the feelings accompanying the engagement of a new generation with the rational, the mythic, the elemental and the spiritual for the first time.

For in play, children can fly, children are Gods, children can become invisible until experience tells them otherwise. Playwork's function is simply to enable children to playfully explore those and all other notions; to learn what is and what is not possible, whilst pushing their individual and collective limits forward. As Sturrock, (2000), emphasises, as playworkers we should continually remind ourselves that in the context of playing it is children who are the sophisticates and it is we who are the primitives.

SECTION 4
THE BASIC FRAMEWORK

THE BASIC QUALITY ASSESSMENT FRAMEWORK

A basic assessment of your practice can be made by reflecting on the Props and Appropriate Intervention Styles you use. It is intended to reflect a short video, or an accumulated picture rather than a snapshot	Never	Sometimes	Often	Normally	Please give brief examples or explanation and be as creative as you can and think about ways children might play with these different mediums
1. Props					
The physical environment I create enables children to play with:					
The Playwork Curriculum					
• fire					
• water					
• air					
• earth					
• identity					
• concepts					
• the senses					
• a varied landscape					
• materials					
• building					
• change					
• focuses					
• choices					
• alternatives					
• tools					
• loose parts					
• risk					
2. Appropriate Intervention Styles					
My intervention style is that I:					
• wait to be invited to play					
• enable play un-interrupted by me to occur					
• enable children to explore their own values					
• leave children to improve their own performance					
• leave the content/intent of play to the children					
• let the children decide why they play					
• enable the children to decide what is appropriate behaviour					
• only organise when children want me to					
subtotal **(a)**					
weighting	1	2	3	4	
TOTAL (Subtotal **(a)** X weighting) **(b)**					
Do you have any comments on the above?					

GRADE ALLOCATION

Allocate yourself one of the following grades according to your amended score.

Grade 1 = 76-100:
Grade 2 = 51-75:
Grade 3 = 26-50:
Grade 4 = 0-25

4

THE BASIC FRAMEWORK

FACTORS THAT MILITATE AGAINST QUALITY

If you have scored 50 or less this may be due to a range of factors that militate against quality over which you have little or no control. This framework will enable these factors to be taken into consideration and may affect your final grading. If you feel that the quality of the provision you operate is affected by any of the following factors, please tick where appropriate. Each tick will add half a point to your TOTAL.

FACTORS THAT MILITATE AGAINST QUALITY – BASIC FRAMEWORK	Tick if appropriate	Please give a brief example or explanation
INTERNAL FACTORS		
• the locality of my provision		
• the quality of the training I have received		
• the size of space we have		
• the type of space we have		
• the number of staff we have		
• provision is shared		
• the level of racism exhibited by children		
• the level of bullying exhibited by children		
• sexism exhibited by children		
EXTERNAL FACTORS		
Significant numbers of children:		
• are over-indulged		
• have to fight for survival		
• have problems at home		
• live in overcrowded conditions		
• are left alone a lot		
• the area is geographically impoverished		
• the area is economically impoverished		
• racism is common in the community		
• sexism is common in the community		
Significant numbers of parents/carers feel that:		
• homework is more important than play		
• play should not be messy		
• children should be kept busy		
Factors that militate against quality subtotal **(c)**		
Do you have any comments on the above?		
Amended TOTAL **(b+ c)** is =		
Action Plan		

GRADE ALLOCATION

Allocate yourself one of the following grades according to your amended score.

Grade 1 = 76-100:
Grade 2 = 51-75:
Grade 3 = 26-50:
Grade 4 = 0-25

4 BASIC FRAMEWORK - DEFINITIONS AND EXPLANATIONS SECTION

Before an assessment using this framework can be carried out effectively, we need to ensure that your understanding of the ideas and the terminology we are using is the same as ours. So this is what we mean by the following terms.

Ideas and Terminology

People often use the same terms to describe different things. This section will attempt to clarify what we mean by the different terms we have used in the framework:

Props

The Playwork Curriculum: Devised by King and Hughes, (see Hughes, 1996b), the curriculum suggests that the essential experiences playworkers make available to children fall into the following categories - The Elements, (Fire, Water, Air, Earth), Identity, Concepts and The Senses. Use the examples as guides only, and be as creative with your children as possible.

The Elements

Fire Experience of fire can be gained through cooking, burning rubbish or simply by enabling children to have small fires. Some play settings give out fire buckets, thus encouraging safety whilst limiting the number of fires to the number of fire buckets. Indoor experience is more limited but can included for example indoor cooking and candle making.

Water Access to water can come in the form of changing the course of streams, water fights, paddling, ice and puddles. Most importantly, access to water should be well supervised, and where appropriate, the depth of water should be kept to a minimum in keeping with the experience.

Air Access to air can come in the form of flying kites, standing in high places, making windmills and model aircraft and watching the effect of wind on trees and water.

Earth Pottery, gardening and mud all give children access to earth. If the play setting has earth banks children will inevitably want to dig holes and caves. If this happens help them to do this safely.

Identity

Children should be enabled to play with their identity, i.e., who they are and what they look like, and with the whole concept of identity. i.e. what does identity mean? Mirrors, face and body paints, make-up, cameras and video can all facilitate this exploration. The favourite however, is the dressing-up box. Play settings that use a dressing-up box should keep it well stocked with every possible item, of all sorts of sizes. It should include everyday clothes, party clothes, uniforms, and the props for imaginary and unusual identities.

Concepts

To make sense of a world in which much of what exists is abstract children need to be able to explore the world of concepts. This doesn't mean that the concepts have to exist in reality. For example democracy can be discussed, as can justice. They and alternatives to them can be played with. Mathematical formulae or signs of the zodiac can be incorporated into the fabric of the play setting. Play clocks and new calendars can represent time. Children have an embryonic awareness of abstracts like religion, philosophy and science from a relatively early age, and need the time and permission to explore them in their own ways.

The Senses

The play setting should stimulate the senses. Music, food, perfumes, colours and views, and different textures do that. Every play setting should have a musical backdrop. Not just 'children's music and nursery rhymes', but all music, in abundance and diversity. The play environment should be a colourful and visually stimulating space, where design subtlety is employed. Playworkers should not just use primary colours or predictable materials. Eibl-Eibesfeldt, (1964), suggested that play is 'scientific research conducted by children'. We should rise to the implied challenge and ensure that the setting facilitates exploration and experimentation. Gardens and/or plants can provide children with a great deal of sensory stimulation. Particularly if there are different types of textures, colours, perfumes and fruit.

Parp!

A Varied Landscape

Play needs a varied environment to be effective. They should contain opportunities to access solitude, height, games with formal/informal rules, slopes, gorges with/without bridges etc.

Materials

Although loose materials are vital to play, access to other materials e.g. cooking equipment, trees, structures, computers etc., is also important.

Building

This refers to construction by the children. There should be building materials; children should be given information regarding building and have access to the tools and techniques needed for building.

Change

Mastery play in particular, requires that children engage in the physical modification of the play space. This could mean anything from re-routing a stream or digging a hole, to building a den or painting a wall.

Focuses

This refers to a feature you will encounter in the ADVANCED Framework, known as neophilia. Neophilia means that children are attracted to play with things they find new, interesting and novel. Children should be provided with features they regard as new, interesting or novel focuses in their play space for them to play with.

Choices

This simple requirement asks if children can make honest and genuine choices about what they do - that there isn't just one thing to do on a take it or leave it basis - a sort of 'football or nothing' situation.

Alternatives

The term alternatives refers to children having access to experiences they would not normally have at home, or in their home locality. For example, step dancing, poetry, trips to the seaside or to an ecological space. However, increasingly for many children alternatives will include outdoor space, dirt and experience of risk.

4

Tools

Mention tools these days and some adults get very nervous. Nonetheless, children need access to the means to create and build as a normal feature of their play experience. Although we wouldn't advocate access to power tools without appropriate supervision, children should be able to have less restricted access to knives, staplers, scissors, hot glue guns, hammers, pliers, saws, including bow saws and hand drills.

Loose Parts

Loose Parts, from Nicholson's Theory of Loose Parts, (1972), refers to anything that can be moved around, carried, rolled, lifted, piled one on top of the other or combined to create interesting and novel structures and experiences. Loose Parts include: wood, containers, shapes, toys, animals, plants and so on.

Risk

Children can only learn to risk assess and avoid unnecessary risks if they know what risk is and have some experience of it. The play setting is ideal for giving children access to experiences that contain risk whilst ensuring that if they do hurt themselves qualified help is at hand. In supervised play settings access to risk has normally been provided through sports and games, climbing, balancing, inter-acting with the elements, travelling through the air at speed, for example bike riding, swinging and using an aerial runway. Sometimes children may hurt themselves, but the injuries are normally very different to those sustained from electric railway lines, roads, multi-storey car parks, rubbish tips, rivers and canals.

Appropriate Intervention Styles

Wait to be invited to play

Playworkers are employed to service and facilitate the children's play experience. They should not expect to play with children unless they are invited by the children to do so. Adults have a tendency to monopolise and manipulate children's play, and should be sensitive and resistant to this, even when they are invited by the children to join in.

Enable play to occur un-interrupted by me

Many play forms, for example imaginative narratives, can only successfully develop if children have the un-interrupted time to get into a play 'state'. What Mears, (1993), called 'being lost in thought'. If the playworker is continually organising, addressing and interrupting children when they are trying to play, it will be a less satisfactory experience for them than it would otherwise be.

Enable children to explore their own values

This is one of those 'as far as it is practicable', standards. Play is a process of 'trial and error' and children will frequently behave in ways that we, as adults, may regard as inappropriate, oppressive or risky, however, this situation is always evolving.

If the content of the play space is good, and if the ambience is supportive and informed, the children will be continually modifying this behaviour as they engage in the play process. Thus rigid and instant application of equal opportunities policies, or other value driven ideas, should be avoided.

Leave children to improve their own performance

Play is essentially an adult-free experience where children have normally learnt their attributes and shortcomings by trial and error. They also learn to improve skills and performance - for example, overcoming a fear of heights, or standing up to a bully. Playworker intervention (or even encouragement) can act to corrupt children's developing judgement, and render them increasingly reliant on the judgement of adults.

Leave the content/intent of play to the children

The nature of the play experience - what children do, how they do it, and why they do it - is a matter for the children. In general, they are the best people to decide what they want to do and why they want to do it. Play should not be seen as entertainment or diversion, but as an integral part of the child's developmental process as a biological organism.

Let the children decide why they play

Studies tend to agree that play is performed for no external goals or rewards. Therefore children should not be induced, offered prizes or be put under other pressures to engage in a particular activity. One good reason for this is that external pressure or inducements may override the child's developing risk-assessment skills and put them in danger. Another is that children may become dependent on adults providing reasons for doing things.

4

Enable the children to decide what is appropriate behaviour

This is another of those, 'as far as is practicable' standards. The play space exists primarily for the children's benefit, as a compensatory measure for loss of other space. For the space to truly belong to the child, then the behaviour that occurs within it (e.g. loud music, smoking, industrial language, fighting, types of games, etc.) should be determined by the children attending and reviewed regularly. However, this approach does have its problems. It can result in a hegemony of under 10's and should be viewed as a matter of principle rather than of dogmatism.

Only organise when children want me too

From time to time children will become bored, uncreative, un-stimulated and generally listless. They may ask you to help by inventing something for them to do - a game, a quiz, a film, a play, a trip or visit. However, playworkers should be sensitive to their own need to please and be needed, and to the child's vulnerability to becoming dependent. You should only organise either when asked by the children or when you judge that such organisation is necessary to give children a break. However, after a spell of organising, resist the temptation until you judge that the same conditions exist again.

THE INTERMEDIATE QUALITY ASSESSMENT FRAMEWORK

An Intermediate Assessment is made by an examination of three areas: Behavioural Modes, Indicators of Play Behaviour and Mood Descriptors. It is intended to reflect a short video, or an accumulated picture rather than a snapshot.	Never	Sometimes	Often	Normally	Please give brief examples or explanation
1. Behavioural Modes					
The children's behaviour as far as possible is:					
• freely chosen					
• personally directed					
• intrinsically motivated					
• in a secure context					
• spontaneous					
• goaless					
• where the content and intent is under their control					
2. Indicators of Play Behaviour					
The children's behaviour contains:					
• diversity of narratives & activity types					
• species & systems interaction					
play types					
• communication					
• creative					
• deep					
• dramatic					
• exploratory					
• fantasy					
• imaginative					
• locomotor					
• mastery					
• object					
• role					
• rough & tumble					
• social					
• socio-dramatic					
• symbolic					
• self-initiated engagement					
• intellectual dialectic					
• play cues/meta communication					
3. Mood Descriptors					
At the play project I operate, children appear:					
• happy					
• independent					
• confident					
• altruistic					
• trusting					
• balanced					
• active or immersed					
• at ease					
subtotal **(a)**					
weighting	1	2	3	4	
TOTAL (Subtotal **(a)** X weighting) **(b)**					
Do you have any comments on the above?					

GRADE ALLOCATION

Allocate yourself one of the following grades according to your amended score.

Grade 1 = 106-140:
Grade 2 = 71-105:
Grade 3 = 36-70:
Grade 4 = 0-35

THE INTERMEDIATE FRAMEWORK

FACTORS THAT MILITATE AGAINST QUALITY

If you have scored 70 or less this may be due to a range of factors that militate against quality over which you have little or no control. This framework will enable these factors to be taken into consideration and may affect your final grading. If you feel that the quality of the provision you operate is affected by any of the following factors, please tick where appropriate. Each tick will add half a point to your TOTAL.

FACTORS THAT MILITATE AGAINST QUALITY – INTERMEDIATE FRAMEWORK	Tick if appropriate	Please give a brief example or explanation
INTERNAL FACTORS		
• the locality of my provision		
• the quality of the training I have received		
• the size of space we have		
• the type of space we have		
• the number of staff we have		
• provision is shared		
• the level of racism exhibited by children		
• the level of bullying exhibited by children		
• sexism exhibited by children		
EXTERNAL FACTORS		
Significant numbers of children:		
• are over-indulged		
• have to fight for survival		
• have problems at home		
• live in overcrowded conditions		
• are left alone a lot		
• the area is geographically impoverished		
• the area is economically impoverished		
• racism is common in the community		
• sexism is common in the community		
Significant numbers of parents/carers feel that:		
• homework is more important than play		
• play should not be messy		
• children should be kept busy		
Factors that militate against quality subtotal **(c)**		
Do you have any comments on the above?		
Amended TOTAL **(b+ c)** is =		
Action Plan		

GRADE ALLOCATION

Allocate yourself one of the following grades according to your amended score.

Grade 1 = 106-140:
Grade 2 = 71-105:
Grade 3 = 36-70:
Grade 4 = 0-35

5 INTERMEDIATE FRAMEWORK - DEFINITIONS AND EXPLANATIONS

As with the BASIC framework, before an assessment using the INTERMEDIATE framework can be carried out effectively, we need to ensure that your understanding of the procedures and the terminology we are using is the same as ours. So this is what we mean by the following terms.

The process is exactly the same as with the BASIC framework. It asks you questions about your practice - but this time in terms of what happens in environments you have created, and about the children's mood there - and depending upon your response, you award yourself points. The 'factors that militate against quality' procedure are also the same.

Ideas and Terminology

This section contains ideas and terminology which is more complex than that contained in the BASIC framework. What follows is our understanding of the terms contained in the INTERMEDIATE framework.

Behavioural Modes

Freely Chosen

Play is defined as behaviour that is freely chosen, personally directed and intrinsically motivated, i.e. performed for no external goal or reward. (PlayEducation, 1984) Ideally, the term free choice should mean exactly that. In reality, however, it should be taken to mean, as free as is practicable given the constraints of the safety of the child. Sylva, (1977), defines play as 'the behaviour in which the sequence of ongoing actions is under the child's intentional control'.

Personally Directed

Play is a process of trial and error and many valuable ideas and pieces of information are acquired. 'Short cutting' this process, e.g. telling a child the 'right way' to hold a hammer or a paint brush will deny children many of these 'first hand' ideas and information. Wherever possible, the child should be in control of 'how' s/he plays. Bruce, (1994), said of play, that 'It actively uses first-hand experiences'.

Intrinsically Motivated

This term means that play is performed for no external goal or reward. (Sylva, 1977) Thus playworkers should avoid contaminating the play process with their own agenda. Koestler, (1964), states, 'The more soiled the purpose of an activity becomes with other motives the less likely that it is play'. Whilst Bruce, (1994), stated that intrinsic motivation, resulting in child-initiated, self-directed activity is valued'. She continued, 'Free flow play (is) intrinsically motivated'.

In a Secure Context

That the child has confidence that any real threat or danger has been minimised. (QA Support Group, 2000).

Spontaneous

Patrick, (1914), defined play as 'Those human activities which are free and spontaneous and which are pursued for their own sake'.

Goalless

Bruner, (1972) stated, 'The play aspect of tool use is underlined by the (child's) loss of interest in the goal of the act being performed and by its pre-occupation with means'.

Where the Content and Intent is under their Control

The child's play not only belongs to the child, but they are also the best judges of their developmental needs. Thus wherever possible, what children do, how and why they do it should be under their control. (Hughes, 2001)

Indicators of Play Behaviour

Diversity of Narratives & Activity Types

The drive to play should be able to manifest itself in the widest possible range of games and activities. Hutt, (1979), for example, argued that 'play is a jumbo category which encompasses a multiplicity of activities'. Bateson and Martin, (1999) wrote that, 'individuals are agents in their own development, seeking out and acquiring experiences, sensations and skills that they will need in later life'.

5

Species & Systems Interaction

Children's play experiences should bring them into contact with the other, non-human species, and with rivers, lakes, seas and other eco-systems. Nicholson, (1972), cited the sea-shore as an exemplary play environment, because of 'its degree of disorder, the availability of mobile components, a large variation of both living and non-living objects, slush (the junction of the water and the sand), etc.

Play Types

Communication Play
Example: name-calling, mime, mickey taking, jokes, facial expression (the play face), gestures, poetry etc. Weininger, O. (1980) 'at play children are constantly talking and thus practising their vocabulary'.

Creative Play
Example: ...where children have access to lots of different creative mediums and tools, where there is plenty of time and where getting messy is not a problem. Koestler, A. (1967) ...a marriage of incompatibles.

Deep Play
Example: Children playing in front of traffic, riding a bike on the parapet of a bridge or through a fire, high tree climbing, especially over rivers or the sea. Geertz, C. (1972) Play in which the stakes are so high, that is...irrational...to engage in it at all.

Dramatic Play
Example: A dramatisation of parents taking children to schools, of a TV show, of a conversation between two people, of a religious or festive event, even a funeral. Garvey, C. (1977) ...play (which) involves recognisable characters and plots or storylines.

Exploratory Play

Example: Engaging with an object or area, and either by manipulation or movement, assessing its properties, possibilities and content. Bretherton, I. (1984) ...includes putting things together, putting one object into another, putting shape blocks into a shape box, or toys in a house; stacking objects on top of one another; making spatial configurations.

Fantasy Play

Example: When children play at a pilot flying around the world, as an owner of an expensive car, or as the catcher of a giant fish. Freud, S. (1959) ...every child at play behaves rather like a creative writer, in that she creates a world of her own, or rather rearranges the things in her world, in a new way which she finds pleasing...she likes to link her imagined objects and situations to the tangible and visible things of the real world.

Imaginative Play

Example: Patting a dog that isn't there, eating food that doesn't exist, or singing into a non-existent microphone. Hayes, C. (1952) 'Performing playful behaviours with non existent materials, apparatus or toys.'

Locomotor Play

Example: Chase, tag, hide and seek, off-ground touch and tree climbing. Van Lawick-Goodall, J. (1968) Behaviour that involves the performance of locomotor patterns in a context that suggests that the only goal is the actual performance of the pattern itself - climbing, swinging, and galloping.

Mastery Play

Example: Fire play, digging holes, changing the course of streams, constructing shelters and growing things. Hendrick, I. (1942) an inborn drive to do and learn how to do, an urge to master the environment.

5

Mood Descriptors

At the play project you operate, children should appear:

Happy they show pleasure or contentment.

Independent they show that they are not depending on authority or control.

Confident they show self-assurance.

Altruistic they demonstrate regard for others as a principle of action.

Trusting they show a firm belief in the reliability or truth of persons or things.

Balanced they show stability of body and mind.

Active or Immersed they are energetic and moving around freely OR absorbed and involved deeply.

At ease they are free of embarrassment, awkwardness, constraint or formality.

6 COMMON QUESTIONS ANSWERED:

Before you begin your self-assessment you should consider the following:

1 question Which framework should I use. Basic, or Intermediate?

answer You should start with the Basic framework and then progress onto the Intermediate. However, you should only move on when you judge that the framework you are on is giving you an accurate assessment of your current practice via the grading you award yourself.

2 question Should I do the self-assessment alone, with another colleague or with my team?

answer Once you have familiarised yourself with each self-assessment framework in turn and feel confident with it and with the language and ideas, you should complete it yourself. The assessment is about your practice.

3 question How often should I use the Quality Assessment process?

answer If you are involved in a two-week holiday playscheme, you should undertake it once in each week.

If you are involved in a scheme that runs from between three and six weeks, you should undertake it once in the middle and once at the end of the project.

If you are involved in a full-time adventure playground or other year round full or part-time project, you should undertake it once every three months.

4 question Do I have to complete the self-assessment form while I am working?

answer You can, but these processes are not intended to be snapshots but rather short videos, so if you prefer you can complete it after you have had a chance to reflect.

5 question Where do I find an explanation of the ideas and terminology?

answer After each of the sections there is an Ideas and Terminology Glossary. Please make yourself familiar with the appropriate one before you complete the related framework. (NOTE. If you feel that the information they offer is insufficient or unclear, please let us know.)

6 question Is there a specific approach on which this framework is based?

answer Yes. They are based on a model of play as an adult-free experience.
To help you to facilitate this try to ensure that:
- neither you nor other adults are physically prominent.
- children's voices predominate.
- children's activity predominates.
- all preparation is completed prior to the children's arrival.

7 question Following the BASIC and INTERMEDIATE processes there is a section called 'factors that militate against quality'. What does this mean?

answer Sometimes children's play provision suffers from a whole variety of factors that can affect the quality of the experience for the child, but which are not to do with your practice. The examples in the sections are self-explanatory but here are few examples of factors that militate against quality and others that do not.

Factors that do not militate against quality: Dogs, dogs faeces, glass, other hazards, rubbish. The site should be cleared of these before opening.

Factors that militate against quality: Too little space, close proximity to pubs, car parks, roads, railway lines, derelict/vandalised buildings, abandoned vehicles, etc.

8 question Following the 'factors that militate against quality' section there is an Action Plan section. What is this for?

answer The Action Plan statement is intended to give you the opportunity - having completed an assessment - to put down a marker about changes you judge are necessary, in terms of your understanding of a particular idea or concept, or regarding a particular aspect of your practice which you feel could be improved.

9 question To what address should I send any feedback?

answer Please forward any comments regarding this assessment process to:
Play Wales, Baltic House, Mount Stuart Square, CARDIFF CF10 5FH,
Tel 029 2048 6050, e-mail mail@playwales.org.uk

7 INTRODUCTION TO THE ADVANCED PLAYWORK QUALITY ASSURANCE FRAMEWORK

The deeper we moved into the development of this document and the processes and thinking it contains, the greater the realisation of the onerous nature of ours and playworkers responsibilities to children in the context of their play.

Play seems to underpin every part of our existence as human beings. Its influence on us as children is immense and fundamental, from both a psychic and a physical perspective. Thus ensuring that the spaces we create for children and the way we operate those spaces and the way we attempt to guarantee their qualitative characteristics becomes vitally important.

This is not simply because it is every child's human right and biological need to experience high quality play in some sort of abstract way, but because play is personal. For better or for worse, each one of us has played, and the child in us insists that we do what we can to ensure that play continues to be available to current and future generations.

In his book, 'The Ambiguity of Play', citing Huttenlocher's work on brain imaging technology, Sutton-Smith, (1997), implies that children under 10 years of age, have at least, twice the potential brain capacity of adults.

This 'over-capacity' is linked to human evolution, because it enables the human brain to retain, what he calls its 'potential variability'. Sutton-Smith suggests that this over-capacity will be more effectively utilised if it is exposed to the diversity of experience through playing.

He also argues that play's role could be in the 'actualisation of brain potential' - making connections in the brain real, rather than possible - 'its function being to save... more of the variability that is potentially there, than would otherwise be saved if there were no play'. (pp. 225-226).

The thrust of his argument, is that if children play their brains will benefit from a phenomenon known as plasticity, and grow larger, than they otherwise would, thus dramatically improving their capacity to store and process information. If this huge neuronal over-capacity is not taken up by the age of ten, it will die off. What Huttenlocher, (1992), calls synapse elimination.

He continues,

'quirky, apparently redundant and flexible responses to experience', i.e., play, result in the uptake of this over capacity, thus ensuring its continued participation in future brain processes, and avoiding problems which Gould, (1996b), suggested were associated with 'rigidification of behaviour after any future successful adaptation'.

What is suggested here, is that not only is play implicated in children's brain development, but in evolution itself. Given our modern industrial context, problems with traffic, pollution and parent's perceptions of 'stranger danger', it makes the delivery of high quality spaces operated by informed and reflective practitioners a matter of urgency, particularly when not to react will leave increasing numbers of children vulnerable to the effects of 'play deprivation'.

Here are some tracts that give us an insight into a play-deprived future:

Huttenmoser et al, (1995), referring to what they describe as 'battery children', attribute play deprivation symptoms to,

'a lack of play, resulting from traffic and parental fears of predatory adults. Battery children are 'often aggressive and whine a lot. By the age of five they are emotionally and socially repressed, find it difficult to mix, fall behind with school work and are at a much greater risk of obesity.'

Chugani's,. (1998), studies on children who have been without play and effectively stimulus deprived, reported,

'mental problems, physical de-sensitisation, and restrictions in brain growth and severe learning difficulties, erratic behaviour, difficulty in forming bonds, depression and withdrawal resembling autistic children or hyperactivity and loss of control, like children with ADD'.

Zuckerman, (1969), referring to extreme levels of neurotransmitters, caused by environmental impoverishment, states,

'inappropriate levels of neurotransmitters were reported to be responsible for an "organism (which) is unsocial or aggressively anti-social'.

Violence and stress can also contribute to play deprivation and lead to neurological and behavioural problems for children. Balbernie, (1999), states:

'A child who has been traumatised will have experienced overwhelming fear and stress. This will be reflected in the organisation of his or her brain, as neurochemical responses to fear and stress have designed it to survive in that sort of environment. By the same token, (a child) who is not being stimulated, by being ...played with, and who has few opportunities to explore his or her surroundings, may fail to link up fully those neural connections and pathways which will be needed for later learning.' (p. 17).

Providing good play environments for children in a context where space is increasingly unavailable for whatever reason, is thus of paramount importance for children's healthy development. But good environments and skilled playworkers are only a part of the equation. We also have to demonstrate that those spaces and workers are being effective in what is increasingly becoming a highly complex and challenging area of endeavour.

Funders need to be convinced and kept on board; parent have to be persuaded to support what we do, and we, the playworkers have to be motivated by the knowledge that we are actually impacting positively on children's lives - that is after all, why playwork exists. This is why the development of a graduated and accessible system that guides our practice towards higher quality and eventually to measurable effectiveness is so essential. The stakes are very high, not least for the children themselves.

That is why, as the development of the ADVANCED framework gets underway we are already aware that the subject of Quality Assessment in playwork is only at its genesis, and that processes which explore the playwork's therapeutic and clinical applications are also developed to better address the needs of the many damaged children who currently use play provision where it is available. Needless to say, the field's co-operation with these developments is vital. Without it development cannot move forward or reach a satisfactory conclusion. Thus provision of the necessary resources - for education and practical training; for travel and accommodation - to facilitate this, particularly in the future, is another important consideration for us. What we have achieved to date is a small but significant step. We trust you will agree and support this project to its successful conclusion.

8 REFERENCES AND BIBLIOGRAPHY

Abernethy, W.D. (1977) <u>Playleadership</u>. London : NPFA

Abernethy, W.D. (1984) in <u>Playwork: Bases, Methods and Objectives.</u>
<u>Proceedings Of PlayEd '84</u>. Bolton : PlayEducation/Bolton MBC

Balbernie, R. (1999) 'Infant Mental Health'. <u>Young Minds Magazine</u>, 39

Bateson, G. (1955) 'A Theory of Play and Fantasy'. <u>Psychiatric Research Reports</u>, No. 2. pp.39-51

Bateson, P.P.G., and Hinde, R.A. (1976) <u>Growing Points in Ethology</u>.
Cambridge : Cambridge University Press

Bateson, P., and Martin, P. (1999) <u>Design for Life</u>. London : Cape

Battram, A. (1997) 'Designing Possibility Space'. PlayEd '97. Ely : PlayEducation

Battro, A.M. (1973) 'Piaget': Dictionary of Terms. Pergamon Press

BBC Horizon (1998) 'Beyond a Joke'

Bennett, E.L., Diamond, M.C., Krech, D., and Rosenzweig, M.R. (1964)
'Chemical and Anatomical Plasticity of Brain'. <u>Science</u>, Vol. 146, Oct

Bexton, W.H., Heron, W., and Scott, T.H. (1954) 'Effects of Decreasing Variation in the Sensory
Environment'. <u>Canadian Journal of Psychology</u>, Vol. 8, No. 2

Bretherton, I. (1984) (ed) <u>Symbolic Play - The Development of Social Understanding</u>.
Orlando : Academic Press

Bruce, T. (1994) 'Play, the Universe and Everything', in Moyles, J.R. (ed),
<u>The Excellence of Play</u>. Buckingham; Philadelphia : Open University Press

Bruner, J.S. (1972) 'Nature and Uses of Immaturity'. <u>American Psychologist</u>, Vol. 27, No. 8

Bruner J.S. (1974) 'Child's Play'. <u>New Scientist</u>, 62, 126

Bruner, J.S.(1976) 'Introduction' to <u>Play: Its Role in Development and Evolution</u>.
New York : Penguin

Bruner, J.S., Jolly, A., and Sylva, K. (1976) <u>Play: Its Role in Development and Evolution</u>.
New York : Penguin

Chilton-Pearce, J. (1980) Magical Child. New York : Bantam Books

Chugani, H. (1998) BBC News 20th April

Cobb, E. (1993) The Ecology of Imagination in Childhood. Dallas : Spring Publications

Connolly, K. (1973) 'Factors Influencing the Learning of Manual Skills by Young Children',
in, R.A. Hinde and J.G. Stevenson-Hinde, (eds)
Constraints on Learning : Limitations and Predispositions. London : Academic Press

Convention on the Rights of the Child, United Nations, September 1990 Conway, M. (1996)
'Puddles - A workshop'. PlayEd '96. Ely : PlayEducation

Conway, M. (1999) 'Quality in Play - A Quality Assurance System for Play Provision in Hackney'.
London : HPA

Egan, J. (1976) 'Object Play in Cats' in Bruner, J.S., Jolly, A,, and Sylva, K. (eds)
Play - Its Role in Development and Evolution. London : Penguin

Eibl-Eibesfeldt, I. (1967) 'Concepts of Ethology and their significance in the study of human
behaviour', in Stevenson, W.W., Rheingold, H.L. (eds)
Early Behaviour : Comparative and Developmental Approaches. New York : Wiley

Eibl-Eibesfeldt, I. (1970) Ethology : The Biology of Behaviour. New York : Holt, Rinehart and Winston

Ellis, M.J. (1973) Why People Play. London : Prentice Hall

Else, P. and Sturrock, G. (1998) 'The playground as therapeutic space : Playwork as healing',
in Play in a Changing Society : Research, Design, Application,
the Proceedings of the IPA/USA Triennial National Conference. Longmont, CO : IPA

Fady, J.C. (1969) Social Play: the choice of playmates observed in the young of the crab eating
macaque. Folia Primat. No. 11, pp.329

Freud, S. (1959) 'Writer and Daydreaming', in J. Strachey (Ed. and Trans.)
The Standard Edition of the Complete Psychological Works of S. Freud (1920-1922), Vol. 18,
London : Hogarth and the Institute of Psychoanalysis

Frost, J.L., and Jacobs, P.J. (1995) 'Play Deprivation : A Factor in Juvenile Violence'.
Dimensions, Vol. 3, No. 3.

Garvey, C. (1977) Play. London : Fontana/Open Books Original

Geertz, C. (1972) 'Deep Play : a Description of a Balinese Cockfight'. Daedalus, No. 101

Geertz, C. (1973) The Interpretation of Cultures. New York : Basic Books

Gordon, C. (1999) 'Riskogenics : an exploration of risk'. PlayEd '99. Ely : PlayEducation

8

Gould, S.J. (1996b) Full House : The Spread of Excellence from Plato to Darwin.
New York : Harmony Books

Groos, K. (1898) The Play of Animals. New York : Appleton

Hall, G.S. (1904) Adolescence: Its Psychology and its Relations to Physiology, Anthropology,
Sociology, Sex, Crime, Religion and Education. Vol. 1. New York : Appleton

Harlow, H.F., and Harlow, M.K. (1962) 'The Effect of Rearing Conditions on Behaviour'.
Bulletin of the Menninger Clinic, 26, 213-224

Harlow, H.F., and Suomi, S.J. (1971) 'Social Recovery by Isolation-Reared Monkeys'.
Proc. Nat. Acad. Sci. USA, Vol. 68, No. 7, pp 1534-1538

Hayes, C. (1952) 'The Ape in our House', in Bruner, J.S., Jolly, A,, and Sylva, K. (eds)
Play - Its Role in Development and Evolution. London : Penguin

Hendrick, I. (1942) 'Instinct and Ego During Infancy'. Psychoanalytic Quarterly, 11, 33-58

Heron, W. (1957) 'The Pathology of Boredom'. Scientific American, 196

Hughes, B. (1984) 'Play a Definition by Synthesis', in Recommendations on Training for Playwork.
London : JNCTP (1985)

Hughes, B. (1988) 'Play and the Environment'. Leisure Manager, Vol. 6, No. 1

Hughes, B. (1996 a.) A Playworker's Taxonomy of Play Types. London : PLAYLINK

Hughes, B. (1996 b.) Play Environments : A Question of Quality. London : PLAYLINK

Hughes, B. (1997b.) 'Towards a Technology of Playwork',
in Proceedings of PLAYLINK/Portsmouth City Council Conference. Portsmouth : PLAYLINK

Hughes, B. (1999a.) 'Does playwork have a neurological rationale?',
in, The Proceedings of PlayEducation '99 Part One. Ely : PlayEducation

Hughes, B. (1999c.) 'Uncensoring Play - Towards an Evolutionary Perspective for Facilitating
Recapitulation'. in the Proceedings of the 14th IPA World Conference, Lisbon, Portugal. IPA: Lisbon

Hughes, B. (2000) 'A Dark and Evil Cul-De-Sac : Has Children's Play in Urban Belfast been
Adulterated by the Troubles?' MA Dissertation. Cambridge : Anglia Polytechnic University

Hughes, B. (2001) Evolutionary Playwork and Reflective Analytic Practice. London : Routledge

Hughes, B. and Williams, H. (1982) 'Talking About Play 1-5'. Play Times, London : N.P.F.A.

Hutt, C. (1979) 'Exploration and Play', in Sutton-Smith, B.(ed), Play and Learning.
New York : Gardener Press

Hutt, S.J., Tyler, S., Hutt, C., and Christopherson, H. (1989) Play, Exploration and Learning.
London : Routledge

Huttenlocher, P.R. (1990) 'Morphometric Study of Human Cerebral Cortex Development'.
Neuropsychologia, Vol. 28, No. 6.
Huttenlocher, P.R. (1992) 'Neural Plasticity', in Asbury, McKhann and McDonald, (eds),
Diseases of the Nervous System 1 : 63-71

Huttenmoser, M., and Degan-Zimmermann, D. (1995) Lebenstraume fur Kinder.
Zurich : Swiss Science Foundation

King, F.M. (1987) 'Play Environment's Criteria' paper. Merseyside Playwork Training Project

King, F.M. (1988) 'Bristol Play Policy' Bristol City Council, Leisure Services

Koestler, A. (1964) The Act of Creation. New York : Dell

Koestler, A. (1967) The Ghost in the Machine. London : Hutchinson

Loizos, C. (1967) 'Play behaviour in higher primates: a review .' in Morris, D. (ed.)
Primate Ethology. Chicago : Aldine Press

Lorenz, K. (1972) 'Psychology and Phylogeny', in Studies in Animal and Human Behaviour.
Cambridge, MA : Harvard University Press

McEwen, B.S. (1999) 'Stress and Hippocampal Plasticity'.
Annual Review of the Neurosciences, 22:105-22

Meares, R. (1993) The Metaphor of Play. London : Jason Aronson Inc.

Milne, J.. (1997) 'Play Structures'. PlayEd '97. Ely : PlayEducation

Moore, R.C. (1986) Childhood's Domain. London : Croom Helm

Morris, D. (1964) 'The Response of Animals to a Restricted Environment'.
Symposium of the Zoological Society of London, 13, 99.

Morris, D. (1967) (ed.) Primate Ethology. Weidenfeld & Nicolson

Nicholson, S. (1971) 'How Not to Cheat Children: The Theory of Loose Parts',
Landscape Architecture, Oct.

Parkinson, C. (1987) <u>Children's Range Behaviour</u>. Birmingham : PlayBoard

Patrick, G.T.W. (1914) 'The Psychology of Play'. Journal of Genetic Psychology, 21, 469-484

Pearce, J.C. (1977) <u>Magical Child</u>. New York : Bantam

Perry, B.D. (1994) 'Neurobiological Sequelae of Childhood Trauma:
Post Traumatic Stress Disorders in Children', in Murberg, M. (ed),
<u>Catecholamines in Post-Traumatic Stress Disorder: Emerging Concepts</u>.
Washington DC : American Psychiatric Association

Perry, B.D. (1995) 'Childhood Trauma. The Neurobiology of Adaptation and Use-Dependent
Development of the Brain. How States Become Traits'. <u>Infant Mental Health Journal</u> Vol. 16, No. 4.

Perry, B.D., Arvinte, A., Marcellus, J. and Pollard, R. (1996) 'Syncope, bradycardia, cataplexy and
paralysis: Sensitisation of an opiod-mediated dissociative response following childhood trauma'.
<u>Journal of the American Academy of Child and Adolescent Psychiatry.</u>

PlayBoard (1997) 'Quality is Play - Quality Assurance Pack'. Belfast : PlayBoard

PLAYLINK (1992) Open Access Play and the Children Act. London : PLAYLINK

PLAYLINK (1997) 'Risk and Safety in Play : The Law and Practice for Adventure Playgrounds'.
London : Routledge

Rennie, S. (1997) <u>The Roots of Consensus</u>. M.A. Dissertation, Leeds Metropolitan University.

Rennie, S. (1999) 'The Isms of Playwork'. PlayEd '99. Ely : PlayEducation

Rennie, S., and Sturrock, G. (1997) Unpublished writings.

Schwartzman, H.B. (1978) <u>Transformations - The Anthropology of Children's Play</u>.
London : Plenum Press

Simpson, M.J.A. (1976) 'The Study of Animal Play', in Bateson P.P.G., and Hinde, R.A.(eds),
<u>Growing Points in Ethology</u>. Cambridge : Cambridge University Press

Sturrock G. (1989) 'Shamanism'. PlayEd ' 1989. Ely : PlayEducation

Sturrock, G. (1993) 'A Metaphysical Journey into the Meaning of Play'.
<u>International Play Journal</u>, Vol. 1, No. 1. January

Sturrock, G. (1997) 'Play is Peace'. Unpublished writing.

Sturrock, G. (1999) 'Personal Communication'.

8

Sturrock, G. and Hughes, B. (2000) 'Personal Communications.

Sutton-Smith, B. (1997) <u>The Ambiguity of Play</u>. Cambridge, Mass. : Harvard University Press

Sylva, K. (1977) 'Play and Learning', in Tizard, B., and Harvey, D. (eds), <u>Biology of Play</u>.
London : Heinemann

van Hooff, J.A.R.A.M. (1972) 'A Comparative Approach to the Phylogeny of Laughter and
Smiling', in Hinde, R.A. (ed), <u>Non-verbal Communication</u>. Cambridge : Cambridge University Press

Van Lawick-Goodall, J. (1968) 'The Behaviour of Chimpanzees:
Animal Behaviour Monographs, Vol. 1., Part 3, Bailliere, Tindall and Cassell

Weininger, O. (1980) 'Play and Early Childhood', in Wilkinson, P.F. (ed), <u>In Celebration of Play</u>.
London : Croom Helm

Zuckerman, M. (1969) 'Theoretical Formulations: 1', in J.P. Zubek (ed),
<u>Sensory Deprivation : Fifteen Years of Research</u>, New York : Appleton-Century-Crofts

Zuckerman, M. (1984) 'Sensation Seeking : A Comparative Approach to a Human Trait'.
<u>The Behaviour and Brain Sciences</u>, 7

9 ACKNOWLEDGEMENTS

Play Wales would like to thank all those who have participated in the process of developing 'the first claim' and the considerable time and dedication given in support of this initiative. The collective vision and faith of the steering group and of the other practitioners involved in tackling new concepts, language, and structures which has resulted in these materials, is testament to their dedication. In particular we would like to thank:

The Steering Group

Barbara Dawe -	Powys Children and Families Forum
Bob Hughes -	PlayEducation - Consultant/Researcher
Brenda Davis -	Childcare/ Out of School Development Officer, Cardiff
Colin Powell -	The Venture, Wrexham
Doug Cole -	Play Officer , Cardiff Play Services
Gill Evans -	Play Wales
Gill James -	Living Proof
Jo Jones -	CYWU, Adamsdown Play Centre, Cardiff
Judy Greenan -	National Playbus Association
Julie Gibbs -	Coleg Glan Hafren, Cardiff
Marianne Mannello -	Valleys Kids, RCT
Mark Sainsbury -	Chwarae Teg Out of School DevelopmentOfficer
Mike Greenaway -	Play Wales
Tony Chilton -	Play Wales

Also

Liz Gibbs - Whizzkids, Llanfyllin, Doreen Aiken - The Venture, Wrexham, Renee Springett - Llansilin Playscheme, Larry Delaney - Rhyl APA, Douglas Taylor - Rhyl APA, Colette Hagerty - Ilan Centre, Nicola Williams - Glyntaff Playscheme, Julie Parson - Valley Kids, Debra Jones - Valley Kids, Cath Ingram - Valley Kids, Katie Greenaway - Bishopston Playscheme, Victoria Harper - Bishopston Playscheme, Ceria Sheeley - Bear Pack, Penarth, John Miller - Bear Pack, Penarth, Danielle Brett - Bear Pack, Penarth, Martine Cucciniello - Bear Pack, Penarth, Laura Shorney - Bear Pack, Penarth, Andrew Davies - Rhyl APA, Amanda Gillespie - Rhyl APA, Jill Owen - Rhyl APA, Annette Allan - Rhyl APA, James Malenga - Splott PlayCentre, Mary Slater - Chwarae Teg, Teresa Ide - Romilly Park Nursery

9

We would also like to thank and acknowledge those organisations who have supported the release of staff from their normal duties, or who have enabled piloting of the Quality Assessment Frameworks in their provision.

We are also very grateful to Mick Conway, the Director of Hackney Play Association, for sharing his rationale for developing 'Quality in Play - A Quality Assurance System for Play Provision' for Hackney. His input was extremely helpful in enabling the steering group to focus their efforts on the requirements of developing a playwork specific process and providing a detailed insight into understanding and identifying the important complex agendas which influence the need for quality assurance.

Our thanks also go to:

European Social Fund - for funding without which this project would not have happened.

National Assembly for Wales - for support for our vision and for financial resources.

Estyn - for sight of their quality frameworks standards.

PlayBoard (Northern Ireland) - for sight of their Quality Assurance process for Out of School Groups.